ETHIOPIA AND THE CHURCH

By

Russell F Johnson

ETHIOPIAN CHURCH .

The Ethiopian or Abyssinian religion, on the Horn of Africa, is individual of the five supposed monophysite Christian churches that renounce the Council of Chalcedon (451) and allure recipe of conviction. The church does not call itself monophysite but instead Tāwaḥedo (Unionite; too spelled Tewahedo), a discussion articulating the merger in Christ of the human and divine natures, to identify itself from the Eastern Orthodox churches, that recognize the formulas endorsed at Chalcedon

For the Tāwaḥedo Orthodox Church of Ethiopia, both Nestorius and Eutyches are heretics. Although formally under the jurisdiction of the Coptic church of Alexandria until 1950, the Ethiopian Orthodox church has managed to retain its indigenous language, literature, art, and music. It expects its faithful to practice circumcision, observe the food prescriptions set forth in the Hebrew scriptures (Old Testament), and honor Saturday as the Sabbath. The church has its own liturgy, including an horologion that contains the daily offices (initially for each of the twenty-four hours of the day), a missal of over fourteen anaphoras, the Deggwā (an antiphonary for each day of the year), doxologies (various collections of nagś hymns), and homiliaries in honor of the angels, saints, and martyrs. The most innovative aspect of this church is the provision in the Deggwā for the chanting of qenē (poetic hymns) in the liturgy. There are several types of qenē varying in number of lines from two to eleven, which one of the clergy usually improvises during the service in keeping with the spirit of Psalms 149:1, "Sing unto the Lord a new song."

Until the Ethiopian mutiny of 1974, the Ethiopian Orthodox Church (the people of that was not completely sixteen million in the early up-to-date, in accordance with the World Council of Churches) had happened a governmental religion protected for one political manager of the country. The ruler's reign had expected legalized by pope's jurisdiction at a scrupulous ceremony place the new ruler vow loyalty to pope's jurisdiction and dedicated himself to uphold the Christian kingdom.

Early History

Historians dissent in appointing a date to the establishment of Christianity into Ethiopia, revolving around at which Ethiopian ruler they judge first selected the faith. The change of the ruler, nevertheless, is a weak evidence of the date of that initiation cause not only was he scarcely with the country's first converts, but likewise cause just before about 960, the kingship transformed hands so repeatedly that the czar was not as consistently Christian as were sure sections of the culture. We bear more skeptical of utilizing the local ethic that the Ethiopian eunuch Qināqis (Acts 8:26–39) was torment education Christianity in Ethiopia as evidence of the country's change. However, we do see that Adulis, the legendary traffic of Ethiopia, and Aksum, the capital, were patronized by Christian merchants from the Hellenistic world because the ancient times of Christianity. Some of these decided skilled, making Christian societies and appealing to to their mythology those accompanying whom they communicated constantly.

Ethiopia formally linked the Christian globe when Frumentius was blessed allure first bishop by Athanasius of Alexandria in about 347. The existing teacher Rufinus (Ecclesiastical History 1.9) narrates us in what way or manner this happened. A certain transport was assaulted while line on individual of the Ethiopian ports. Of the voyagers, only two Syrian boys from Tyre (up-to-date-epoch cold Lebanon), Frumentius and Aedesius, out dying. The guys were captured to the mansion, place the king fashioned Frumentius welcome desk and Aedesius welcome cupbearer.

Frumentius secondhand welcome influence in the hall to help the construction of an eloquence for one Christians in the city. This center was again secondhand as a school where babies, even those from non-Christian kins, came near accept conscientious education. As promptly as two together foreigners taken their privilege, Frumentius make use of Alexandria to request the priest skilled to ordain a clergyman for the Christians in Ethiopia. Athanasius at which point chose Frumentius expected the clergyman of Aksum. Rufinus suggests that he taken this news "from the opening of Aedesius himself," the one enhanced a monk in Tyre. Even though Rufinus, like different writers, calls the country India, skilled is certainly that the tale handles Ethiopia. A answer from the Arian ruler, Constantius II (r. 337–361), to the rulers of Ethiopia, Ezana (ʿĒzānā) and Sazana, having to do with Frumentius is surviving in Athanasius's Apology to Constantine (Patrologia Graeca, ed. by J.-P. Migne, 25. 636–637). From Ezana's rule to the middle of the twentieth of one hundred years, the head of the Ethiopian chapel waited a Copt. It was only in the twentieth centennial that an Ethiopian, Bāsleyos (1951–1970), was blessed elder. It must be eminent, still, that the Coptic cosmopolitan was administrative generally of otherworldly and religious matters.

Medieval Period

The Ethiopian chapel accepted many important often quickly betwixt the divide into four equal parts and the seventh of one hundred years. It energetically interpreted a lot of Christian history from Greek. This contained the Old Testament from the Septuagint and the New Testament from the Lucianic rewriting (the Greek Bible corrected by Lucian of Antioch, d. 312) secondhand in the Syrian religion. The Ethiopian Bible of eighty-individual books contains procedure of Jubilees and procedure of Enoch, two books that have happened maintained in their wholeness only in Ethiopic. The Synodicon (a group of church law), the Didascalia Apostolorum (a faith order), the Testament of Our Lord, and the Qalēmenṭos (an fateful book ascribed to Clement of Rome) are too some the Ethiopian accepted doctrine. The number of churches and monasteries more evolved fast. Traveling through Ethiopian regions in the sixth centennial, a Greek friar, Cosmas Indicopleustes, was aroused to visualize churches far and wide.

happened submitted that the Rule of Pachomius and the religious manuscripts of the Fathers in the Qērelos (containing handwritings from Cyril of Alexandria, Epiphanius, and others.) were influenced to Ethiopia for one supposed Nine Saints the one arose the Hellenistic or Mediterranean planet, containing Egypt, in the sixth or seventh centennial. But one common people hikers and anchorites (in the way that Abbā Yoḥannes Kamā) the one got near Ethiopia much former than the Nine Saints power have led bureaucracy in addition to various added everything. Our real information about the Nine Saints is not immovably located in spite of they are well prize in pope's jurisdiction as the founders of monasticism in Ethiopia.

Unfortunately for the trusty, the young faith endured infringement and badgering by Islam, starting in the eighth of one hundred years. Locally, excessively, a servant monarch of individual of the provinces, Gudit, nauseated and demolished the Christian culture, concreting the way for another empire, the Zāgwē (1137–1270).The Zāgwē kings were more concerned in mythology than in campaigning. Many of bureaucracy were friars in addition to shahs, and the last four of the regime are, really, among the holy persons of pope's jurisdiction. The construction of the various rock-cut churches in Lāstā (main Ethiopia) is attributed to bureaucracy.

The supposed Solomonic regime, that search out defeat bureaucracy, would boast of allure asserted descendance from Solomon of Israel, while the Zāgwē tried to copy the religious places in their own land, lifework their capital Roha (later Edessa), their river Yordanos (later Jordan), thus.In 1270 the priesthood, experienced by Takla Hāymānot, the founder of the Monastery of Dabra Libanos (in Shewa), and Iyyasus Mo'a, the founder of the Monastery of Ḥayq Esṭifānos (in Amhara), hookedup accompanying Yekunno Amlāk to destroy the Zāgwē and to raise the Solomonic regime. Although the Solomonic kings acted not continually celebrate pope's jurisdiction's education, it was nevertheless all along this ending that inborn conscientious article grew, and Christianity spread into the cold and west through the exertions of the monks of Dabra Libanos of Shewa, the twelfth neburāna ed, preferred by the cosmopolitan in accordance with the number of the apostles.

The Jesuits' Enterprise

The Portuguese arrived help pope's jurisdiction in allure war against Islam accompanying the arrogance that the missing flock, pope's jurisdiction of Ethiopia, would return to the Roman Catholic Church. The Ethiopians, nevertheless, were never ready to abandon their conviction. The pressure of the Jesuits, nevertheless, that begun accompanying messengers shipped by Pope Julius III (1487–1555), persisted as far as the seventeenth centennial, when they achieved in adapting Emperor Suseneyos (r. 1607–1632) to Catholicism. In 1626 a Catholic founder, Alphonsus Mendez, emanated Rome, and the ruler circulated a decree that welcome subjects bear attend welcome own instance.

However, the wide-ranging change that Mendez tried to introduce into the timeworn conscientious habits of the country with its own government met with hard opposition. Led for one austere leaders, tens of chiliads of the trusty were torment. The Catholic messengers were finally requested to leave, and the ruler was assassinated, in spite of he had abdicated royalty to his offspring Fāsiladas (r. 1632–1667). Fāsiladas was unstinting accompanying the Jesuits even though that they had attempted to defeat him by seeking individual of welcome brothers.

Even though the Jesuits abandoned, the dispute preventing from their belief of two together natures of Christ resumes to the, taking a local integrity and constituting gap in the Ethiopian chapel. Overtly, this dispute is focused on the religious meaning of qeb'at, ointment (Acts 10:38), and bakwr, senior (Rom. 8:29), when used to Christ the Messiah, the only Son of God. But those the one produced these questions were plainly attempting to show the monophysites the association of a dogma of individual character in Christ, by illustration their consideration to the specific demeanor of the psychology of humankind in him and allure inferior position vis-à-vis welcome sanctity. For individual group, the Kārroch, or Tāwaḥedo (the Unionists of Tegrāy), whose position the church has grasped formally because 1878, ointment wealth the merger of sanctity accompanying benevolence:

Christ, the one is the balm and the blessed, enhanced the instinctive Son of God in welcome benevolence through this cause. For the Qebatoch (unctionists of Gonder and Gojam), sacrament method that Christ in welcome benevolence enhanced the open Son of God through the ointment of the Holy Spirit: God the Father is the anointer, the Son the blessed, and the Holy Spirit the balm. The triennial group, the Ṣaggoch (adoptionists of Shewa), the one are blamed of inclined to a type of behavior Catholicism, trust that Christ in welcome benevolence enhanced the Son of God by grace through the ointment of the Holy Spirit either in Mary's interior at the Annunciation or at the initiation.

district Catholicism, trust that Christ in welcome benevolence enhanced the Son of God by grace through the sacrament of the Holy Spirit either in Mary's interior at the Annunciation or at the initiation. They call the occasion when he enhanced the Son of God by grace a tertiary beginning for Christ, concerning the endless beginning from the Father and the worldly beginning from Mary, therefore the blasphemy of the three births convicted at the Council of Boru Meda in Welo (principal Ethiopia) in 1878. The Ṣaggoch furiously fight the desire that Christ enhanced the open Son of God in welcome benevolence. They are, nevertheless, in the youth.

The Church outside Africa

Designed to express allure religious communication and to act the services in the local education, the Ethiopian religion is rigidly local and nationwide. In allure past it has not committed in some missionary actions further the boundaries that governmental commanders demanded expected regions of their ancestors. King Kālēb's journey to Najrān (pertaining to the south Arabia) in about 525, to rescue the Christians from the affliction of a Jewish monarch and to rearrange the Christian societies skilled, grant permission not be considered maintained project by pope's jurisdiction outside Ethiopia. Even the Ethiopian churches in the Holy Land take care of not be irregularities to this factual case, because they were built to do Ethiopian national the one haunted the religious places in Palestine and Egypt.

In the 1950s the Ethiopian religion was met accompanying a different challenge. The local religion was named upon to put oneself in the place of another the need for educational and ethnic correspondence of the downtrodden dirty public in Africa and the Americas. Churches accompanying the term Abyssinian as some their name begun to arise in these shore. Although the classical link middle from two points the Ethiopian religion and these churches is deficient, and the Ethiopian faith was not economically, educationally, and with regard to the welfare of mankind until the challenge, delegates involving priesthood were shipped from Ethiopia to East Africa (still under British rule), the Caribbean domain, and North America.

The certain questions were by what method to entice the common people to an African faith and by means of what to accommodate the with regard to the welfare of mankind alien chapel aids to English-expressive societies in Africa and the Americas, containing the question of rebaptism. The compromise attained search out hire few parts of the ceremony in Ge'ez and conduct the rest in English. This compromise was not only insufficient to two together pope's jurisdiction experts and congregations, but it again intended preparation the priesthood, Ethiopians and non-Ethiopians alike, in Ge'ez and English. In spite of various questions, pope's jurisdiction is recuperating, exceptionally in the West Indies and the Caribbean (such as, Jamaica, Guyana, Trinidad, and Tobago).

Primary denominations
The Ethiopian Kale Heywet (Word of Life) Church, a charming Evangelical Protestant classification accompanying Pentecostal and Baptist ancestries. It is guide the Sudan Interior Mission, an assorted arranging, and has an Eritrean arm.
The Ethiopian Evangelical Church Mekane Yesus (Place of Jesus), a Lutheran classification that contains a Presbyterian-tendency council. The Eritrean Evangelical Church Mekane Yesus is the Eritrean Lutheran arm concerning this Evangelical Protestant name.

The Ethiopian Lutheran name is the best non-combined Lutheran Christian classification (visualize list of Christian denominations according to the highest authority of appendages). The Evangelical Lutheran Church of Eritrea, a Lutheran classification that linked the Lutheran World Federation in 1963.
The Ethiopian Full Gospel Believers' Church, a Pentecostal name accompanying Mennonite influence.
The Meserete Kristos (Christ Foundation) Church, a Mennonite classification accompanying Pentecostal influence.
Christian Brethren
Some P'ent'ay communities—especially the Mekane Yesus Lutheran Church for example—have happened affected apiece Orthodox Tewahedo churches, that shows the main usual Ethiopian and Eritrean Christian mathematical, except for ultimate part are very Pentecostal in their worship and dogma.

Other denominations
Ammanuel Baptist Church
Misgana Church of Ethiopia
Assemblies of God – Pentecostal
Hiwot Berhan Church (Light of Life Church)
Emnet Kristos
Berhane Wongel – Gospel Light
Ethiopian Addis Kidan Baptist Church
Evangelical Church of Eritrea
Lutheran Church of Eritrea
Middle East General Mission
Seventh-epoch Adventist Church[12]
Anglicanism is presented in Ethiopia and Eritrea apiece Episcopal Church in Jerusalem and the Middle East and Episcopal Anglican Province of Alexandria; Ethiopia and Eritrea are two together indiscriminate the Diocese of Egypt, that further involves additional nations in the Horn of Africa in addition to the North Africa domain. There are two Episcopal churches in Ethiopia, individual is in Addis Ababa and the different in Gambela, while in Eritrea skilled are no regularly conducted congregations at the present.
Copy
Stats:

NOTES

NOTES